"Kevin's understanding o on the market allows schools to focus on the bigger picture - improving student outcomes."

John Myers
Director of Marketing & Training
Haskell Furniture

"When it comes to the impact furniture can have on learning outcomes, there is no better source to guide you through the process. This book is filled with case studies of how other schools have made it a priority to improve the learning environment for their students."

Katy Bainbridge
President
Align, Assess, Achieve

"*Creating Better Learning Environments* is a practical guide that every educator should read and be striving toward."

Damon Norris
Director of Member Services
Arizona Charter Schools Association

"The habitat within which humans learn demands attention, and Kevin's intention to support and guide is evident within this book."

Jonathan Matta
Designer

1

CREATING BETTER
LEARNING ENVIRONMENTS
FURNITURE CONCEPTS TO ENHANCE
STUDENT OUTCOMES

KEVIN STOLLER
Foreword by Stephan Cooke

ISBN-13: 978-1539385684
ISBN-10: 153938568X

Library of Congress Control Number: 2017916413
CreateSpace Independent Publishing Platform,
North Charleston, SC

Shoop Media, LLC
5625 N. High Street, Suite 1
Worthington, OH 43085
877-746-6785
www.shoopmedia.com

Dedication

The educators that strive everyday
to provide the best learning experience
for their students. The ones that
never take no for an answer,
encourage failure, and challenge people
to get out of their comfort zone.

Acknowledgements

This book was a collaborative effort among the staff of our company, **Kay-Twelve.com**. *Creating Better Learning Environments* is at the core of what we do every day and this book is a great example of our team commitment.

I would like to specifically acknowledge:

Stephanie Robertson for her work creating renderings of spaces to bring the concepts to life. Her work researching best practices combined with our real world experience helps visualize what we are talking about.

Bob Roche brought over 30 years of industry experience to provide knowledge of what has worked and hasn't worked as school environments have evolved.

Yolanda Jackson has always been willing to take on any task that we needed from research to coordinating customer feedback.

Kim Taylor provided valuable insight and review of the work in this book. She found many examples and additional insights that helped us refine the pages before you.

Linda Donaldson played an integral role in keeping us on task and providing the guidance on what it takes to get a book into publication. I enjoyed our conversations and the common bond we share as alumni of Miami University in Oxford, Ohio.

I am extremely proud of the team we have built and the values that we strive to uphold. We hope the work in this book truly makes an impact in educational environments around the world.

I'd also like to thank my wife, **Darci**, for the encouragement to continue with this project even though it took time away from the family. She listened to hours of my ramblings about the state of education as I was putting thoughts together in the creative process. I love you and hope this book contributes to the movement of creating better learning environments for our own children.

Contents

Continued on Next Page ➤

FOREWORD

An important lesson I learned while pursuing my Bachelors of Science degree in Elementary Education was that the critical path to student success is for teachers to connect subject matter and student interest. As basic as this concept is, in recent years we've seen many examples of just the opposite – a disconnect or breakdown in learning. One prevalent reason, I believe, is current teachers' abilities to balance the complicated "classroom climate" which includes the social, emotional, and physical aspects of the classroom.

While classroom performance often focuses on teacher to student communication and the emotional well-being of the students, there is often a failure to incorporate the physical considerations of the classroom which can make an environment less conducive to learning. As critical as the furniture can be to the student's comfort and well being in the learning environment, it is more often the component that gets the least amount of consideration.

Experts agree that when students interact with each other and have a chance to voice their opinions to their peers, they work out issues among themselves. Collaboration results in a deeper understanding of the material which, in turn, leads to better test scores.

In my teaching experiences, I worked in a variety of classroom settings and taught many different types of students. I was always amazed and disappointed to see the disengagement of many of the children as they sat in conventional desks, with a hard plastic seat and limited space to move to find personal comfort. I also started to recognize that students have different learning needs and body types, yet I saw them being crammed into stationary desks all lined up in the same direction - never to be moved or changed. That old static furniture model limits student engagement.

Fast forward some 30 years to my new job as a sales manager selling contract furniture. I was again amazed to see classroom environments had not changed. Children still sat in their stationary desks all in tight rows facing the teacher and the front. What really struck a chord is, considering all the research and resources that have gone into teaching and education, the physical classroom environment has evolved little.

In the last several decades, we have seen the demographics and characteristics of students change drastically. Especially with the increase of the number of students per classroom, assimilating children with special needs, larger and earlier developing students, and rapid changes in technology – still classrooms have seen little change.

Ironically, outside the school setting you will see companies invest in wellness, the study of ergonomics, and the constant updating of office furniture – all to the ensure the comfort and productivity of its workers. Yet, in our classrooms, you still have students sitting for up to seven hours a day with minimal consideration of their comfort.

Often the outlet for student discomfort is displayed as antsy behavior, boredom, squirming, and even sleeping. Hampering the learning process, these behaviors are disruptive and, in effect, create disconnects between teaching and learning.

My passion for educating students has always been a part of my life. Throughout my career I've worked with children, started a non-profit organization teaching environmental education to inner-city students, mentored, and started a cross-country team at a local elementary school.

After long discussions with my wife, I recently explored options for getting back to working with students full-time, hopefully having a positive impact on how children learn. In my search, one of the first people I contacted was Kevin Stoller who I knew from my furniture days. I reached out to Kevin to hear his experience and insight in the education market.

What started out as a "catch up" chat quickly turned into a long conversation about education and the direction we both see it going. More importantly, we discussed some of the shortcomings we were seeing in the school setting.

One thing Kevin and I vehemently agreed upon was how the classroom settings in most schools are dated and archaic. We recognized our mutual passion for education and the desire to have an impact on making things better for students. Our initial conversation turned into ongoing get-togethers.

Ultimately they led to my joining his team at Kay-Twelve, because my personal beliefs were in line with Kevin's commitment to creating better learning environments.

It is interesting where life can take you, circling back to my original goal to impact children and how they learn. However, my influence is not seen using a text book, but with creating a healthy physical space that can enhance the learning process. I am excited to impact, through this book and my work at Kay-Twelve, a greater amount of students and schools.

So what does it mean to "create better learning environments"? In this book you will find descriptions of different learning styles and case studies of schools attempting to create better learning environments. Most have been successful, but it is also good to hear the lessons learned about what they would have done differently.

The overall goal in of this book is for education experts to recognize the need to embrace different learning styles to allow every student to thrive. By doing so, the physical space can have a positive impact on this process.

Teachers will hopefully consider furniture a learning tool and/or an extension of their teaching methodology. They can ditch the "lecture" approach and offer flexible, collaborative environments that allow them to become "coaches" roaming the classroom, acting as a trusted advisor and encouraging "self-directed" learning. Furniture can enhance the learning process and impact how students engage, collaborate, and ultimately strengthen their interest in learning.

The journey of the author has been to learn best practices from educators and draw on his experiences at Kay-Twelve to share this journey with the reader. This book is written for the educators and administrators that have the same commitment to create an environment that is conducive to giving the students the best opportunity to learn.

I hope you see the value in this journey. Creating better learning environments is not as daunting as one would think, but it all starts with the drive to make it a reality.

Stephan Cooke

Introduction

At the heart of Creating Better Learning Environments is the premise that students of all ages learn differently, and it is the job of educators to adapt to each student's learning styles. This book is a practical guide to help educators make this a reality through a proven process that many schools around the world have implemented.

The wording of the title was chosen after careful thought.

- **Creating** is meant to be a verb, an action that is ongoing and is never meant to be in a completed state.

- **Better** signifies improvement and not accepting the status quo. Striving for progress instead of perfection.

- **Learning** is the magical moment when you can see the student comprehend. We wanted to pinpoint the AHA! moments when the learning actually occurs and how to maximize those learning situations.

- **Environments** takes the idea of learning beyond just the classroom. A large portion of this book is spent on classrooms, but we want to look at a school as a facility of learning opportunities in each square foot - inside and outside of the building.

Throughout this book we provide examples of how other schools intentionally sought to improve their learning environments. By sharing best practices, roadblocks, and lessons learned to assist you on your journey.

Not all schools have the opportunity to start a new facility from scratch or undergo major renovations, so the majority of this book will show you how to better utilize and enhance your current facility.

This book begins and ends with the primary purpose of matching a student's environments with his or her dominant learning styles. However, the results of this approach lead to other important benefits such as community engagement, school reputation, and the recruiting and retaining of students and educators.

Few people outside the school get glimpses of the education staff in action, but instead create their perceptions based on the physical environment they see when they visit the school during non-school hours.

It is our intent that this book guide you through your process and help you overcome the most common obstacles. Some of these ideas require funding, but many of them only require effort. Thank you for being a leader and advocate to better educate the students in your community!

Kevin Stoller
June 2017, Worthington, Ohio

PART ONE

HOW WE LEARN

I've been in thousands of classrooms throughout my career. The vast majority of them look like this:

Students sit in their assigned seats in straight rows. The teacher is at the front of the classroom near his desk to start the session. He has a front board that is either dry erase, Smartboard, projector, LCD screen, chalkboard - or a combination of these.

The students are expected to pay attention, sit still, watch the board, take notes, and be quiet - unless they raise their hands and wait to be called on. When the bell rings, they go to their next class and repeat throughout the day.

Sound familiar?

However, there is a movement going on today in education, a literal movement. I've had the privilege to witness classrooms that look more like this:

Students come into the class excited and pick where they want to learn. There is noise coming from all directions. The teacher gets the students' attention in the middle of the classroom and everyone swivels, loosely forming a circle around her to make eye contact.

The instruction is brief and to the point, the students get the game plan for the day and break off into groups of 4-5 and make space to interact. Again, eye contact is made, this time between peers as they communicate on their work.

One student breaks off from the group to work on their portion of the project. The teacher moves throughout the room and challenges the students on their thought process. Several times throughout the class period, she gets everyone's attention by sharing info from her hand-held device to the monitors positioned around the room.

One student jumps out of his chair and paces, then points to the screen that a classmate is sharing from her device. The room is buzzing, maybe even considered loud. The student that broke away, now has headphones on, but is re-joining his group after sharing what he created.

The class period is half-way done and the teacher starts reminding groups that they'll be presenting in a few minutes. Time is up and the first group shares their screen with the rest of the class. The students swivel their chairs to watch the presenter, their own devices put down.

One student scoots closer to hear and see better. Two other groups share their progress and a discussion ensues. With two minutes left, the teacher gets back in the middle of the classroom, reminding students of the deadline and the work they need to do that evening. The bell rings and a few students remain to ask questions as the discussions continue into the hallway.

With the integration of technology into the classroom, this second example is now a reality for many schools all over the country. Whether the first or second example describes your school, this book is written for you. The **Early Adopters** of new technology, furniture, and educational tools have paved the way for the **Early Majority**. Lessons were learned, corrections have been made, and we are now seeing the **Early Majority** joining the revolution of improving learning environments.

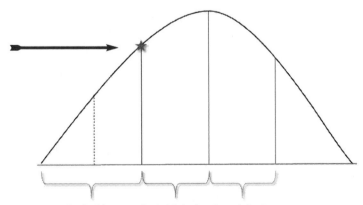

Early Adopters Early Majority Late Adopters

The Challenge

The education system is more complicated than ever. Various student needs, demands from society, parents, and government entities. Additional constraints may be old buildings and inadequate teaching space due to more students per classroom. The staff and teachers are asked to do more with similar - or even less - resources. There may be times when you feel like you are in a no win situation and the thought process is focused on surviving, instead of thriving.

The Opportunity

We get it. None of this is easy, but it is an enormous opportunity to make positive impact on students' lives. We all have the desire to be a positive influence and drive change within the education community. It only takes one voice to challenge, inspire, and lead in a common goal of creating better learning environments.

Learning Environment Catch-words

The idea of changing the learning environment is not new. Different terms and buzzwords have been used to describe trends:

- **21st Century Learning (*As of 2017, 17% of the 21st Century is now HISTORY. Can we stop using this term?*)**
- **Flexible Learning Spaces**
- **Student-Centered Learning**
- **SEL (*Social and Emotional Learning*)**
- **Collaborative Learning**
- **4C's (*Creativity, Collaboration, Communication, Critical Thinking*)**

When it comes down to it, the main purpose of education is to help students maximize their potential. For the purposes of this book, we are going to simplify all the catch-words and just focus on making things *better*. To do this, we need to start with the basics and focus not on the status quo, but on how can we improve. In addition, the educational landscape continues to be more complex - from student needs, testing requirements, and a changing educational population.

With all these changes, there is a need to implement a proven process. Some schools have engaged with educational consultants, while others have self-implemented with resources such as this book.

Tony Wagner talks about this in his book **Most Likely to Succeed**, referring to the improvement process as "educational Research & Development." The idea of many schools trying different tactics to improve the educational outcomes.

LEARNING STYLES

Let's start by looking at the different learning styles of individuals. Each student has a predominant learning trait - but will exhibit one or more of the six basic learning styles - **Auditory, Visual, Physical, Verbal, Solitary or Social.**

1. AUDITORY

These learners need to clearly hear information.

The students that need a quiet space when having a conversation, or to be close to the person speaking during a presentation. Without proper acoustics, this type of learner can get distracted or frustrated.

2. VISUAL

If these learners don't see it, they don't remember it.

Everything visual is a stimulus - from what is on the walls, down to students' personal workspace. They learn from reading, viewing presentations, and graphical representations.

Learning Styles

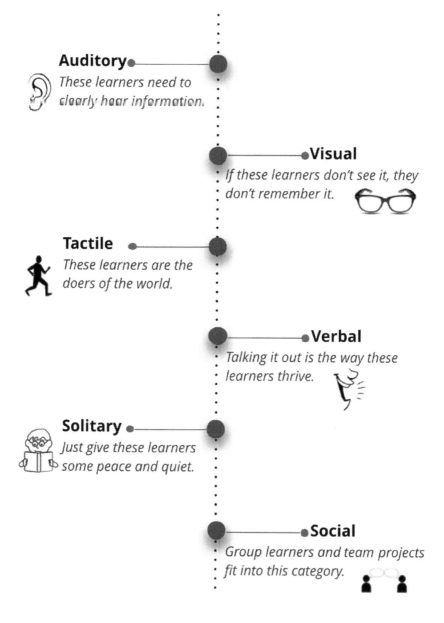

Auditory
These learners need to clearly hear information.

Visual
If these learners don't see it, they don't remember it.

Tactile
These learners are the doers of the world.

Verbal
Talking it out is the way these learners thrive.

Solitary
Just give these learners some peace and quiet.

Social
Group learners and team projects fit into this category.

3. TACTILE

These learners are the doers of the world.

These students need to get involved and learn by trial and error. The space they require can sometimes be messy. It may necessitate utilizing outdoor space to release their full mental potential. Makerspaces are also being utilized to engage these types of learners. More info on Makerspaces in the Bonus Section of this book.

4. VERBAL

Talking it out is the way these learners thrive.

By allowing interaction and creating collaborative situations, the verbal learner gets to brainstorm and figure things out by verbalizing his thought process. These are also the learners that fit the adage, "You don't really know it until you can teach it to others."

5. SOLITARY

Just give these learners some peace and quiet.

Let them get in their own zone to figure things out without distractions. Whether they need a way to break away from the group, close the door, or have some privacy screens – it is up to the leaders of the school to provide the outlets for solitary learners to excel. With the increased focus on collaboration, these learners may need special time dedicated to their needs.

6. SOCIAL

Group learners and team projects fit into this category.

The ability to work through it with others is the toughest environment to create, since it requires many variables and options for the students. This is especially true when technology is introduced. If everyone is working on their own devices, technology to share the info with the group is a challenge.

Do you know which type of learner you are?

Do you know which type of learner your students' are?

This is valuable information that can help you tailor the needs of each student.

Download the planning guide that includes more information about surveys and a cheat sheet on the learning styles.

http://www.kay-twelve.com/bookplanningguide

PART TWO

MATCHING LAYOUTS
TO
LEARNING STYLES

Classroom Layouts
that Match Learning Styles

This chapter illustrates, with both 2D diagrams and 3D views, the six basic types of classroom layouts and some variations on them.

To better plan your spaces, we explain how the layouts do, *and sometimes don't*, accommodate different learning styles.

The six styles shown are:

1. **Traditional Layouts**

2. **New Traditional Layouts** *with two variations*

3. **Collaborative Layouts** *with four variations*

4. **Ultimate Flexibility Layouts** *with three variations*

5. **Team-Based Layouts**

6. **Student Choice Layouts**

1 . Traditional Layouts

This traditional classroom design has been used for approximately 150 years. The design of rows with a teacher providing a lecture is based on the same principles of the industrial revolution. Maximize efficiency and space. One teacher can teach many. Rows are uniform and built as utilitarian spaces, meant to house as many students as possible.

Unfortunately, this is still the most popular classroom design. However, it only matches up with a few of the learning styles, assuming you have one of the preferred seats toward the front and middle of the classroom. It also provides ample choice for the students that do not want to maximize their learning experience, with many seats poorly positioned to hear or see the main subject. These students typically sit in the back of the classroom when given the choice.

The furniture in the traditional style is typically heavy chair & desk combinations. Many times called combo desks, these are typically chairs that are attached to the work surface. There may or may not be a book rack for storage underneath the seat. The seats could be made out of wood, hard thermoplastic, or soft molded plastic. The work surface, which was traditionally wood, may also be a molded thermoplastic or laminate top.

Although the materials have changed over the years, the concept is still the same. The furniture is intentionally made to be set up in rows and very difficult to move into a different configuration. They are heavy to move and built to last a long time, which has proven to be successful. It is common for these to last 25-50+ years.

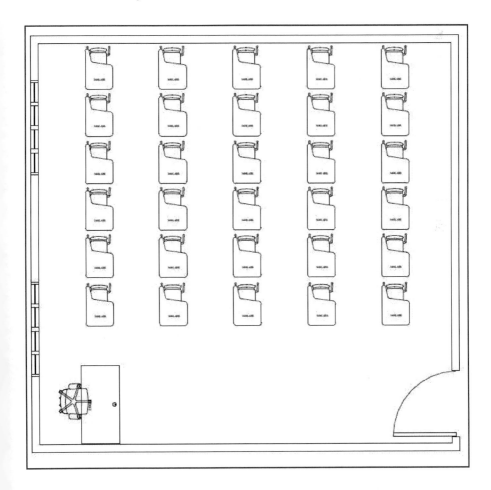

Traditional Layout with combo desks in tight rows and teacher at the front of classroom.

Traditional Layout 3D view emphasizing the distance away from the board for those at the back.

2. NEW TRADITIONAL LAYOUTS

The idea of the **New Traditional** is meant to give more flexibility to the traditional layout. The furniture is primarily kept in the same configuration, straight rows facing forward, but the main difference is the chair and desk are no longer connected.

This slight change in design opens up many new possibilities into the classroom. Because it is lighter weight and easier to move the chair and desk individually, group work now becomes an option. Ask teachers that have this style of furniture and describe how easy it is to move throughout the day, and you may get a description like the one below:

> *"Moving the chairs and desks is a time consuming and disruptive task. Some students have a hard time lifting and moving the chair and desk. You hear the noise as they drag them across the floors and see the markings of the damaged floor."*

This does not stop some educators from reconfiguring the classroom based on the subject at hand. Some do set the classroom up for discussion mode and then move into group work.

However, the most common result is one configuration is set for an extended period of time, many times for the duration of the school year.

So if a teacher is most comfortable with lecture mode, they are set up in rows and stay that way. If the teacher is emphasizing group work, they remain in groups of 4 - even when the learning topic would provide a better learning experience in a different configuration.

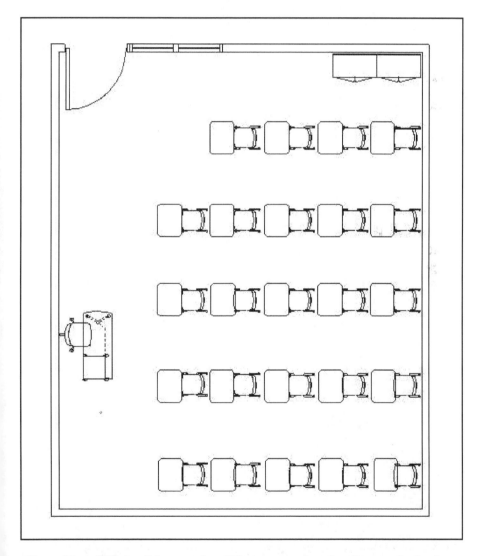

New Traditional Layout with separate desks and chairs.

New Traditional Layout with separate desks and chairs.

The following pictures are an example of the New Traditional furniture set up in group configurations. Depending on the shape of the desk, these can be groups of 2, 3, 4, 5 or 6. This configuration is ideal for project based learning and collaborative assignments. The weaknesses include poor positioning for visual and auditory learners. Many will have their backs to the material or the speaker, making it difficult to see or hear.

New Traditional Layout with desks and chairs in groups.

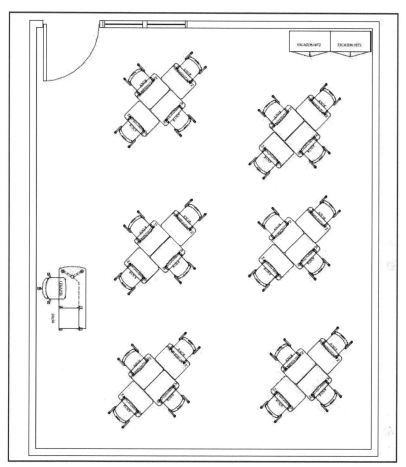

New Traditional Layout with desks and chairs in groups.

3. COLLABORATIVE LAYOUTS

The Collaborative Layout is similar to New Traditional, with a few major differences. The non-rectangular shapes present less uniformity in the room and saves space in a grouped setting.

Selecting the right shape of student desk will depend on the goals of collaboration and technology used in the classroom. Many of the furniture decisions are based on whether the school is **1-1** *(commonly referred to as one-to-one if the school has one electronic device per student)* and which technology platform is being used. The most common are Chromebooks, Macbooks, or iPads.

31

Some 1-1 schools are able to keep all the student work digitally while others commonly have a device and a pad of paper. This will require a larger work surface that can influence the shape and size of student desks.

Different shapes also have an affect on the capacity of each classroom. The **triangular desks** shown below save space for groups of 4, preventing any wasted space between students. In contrast, they work poorly for groups of 5. A hexagon shape may be more ideal for those requirements.

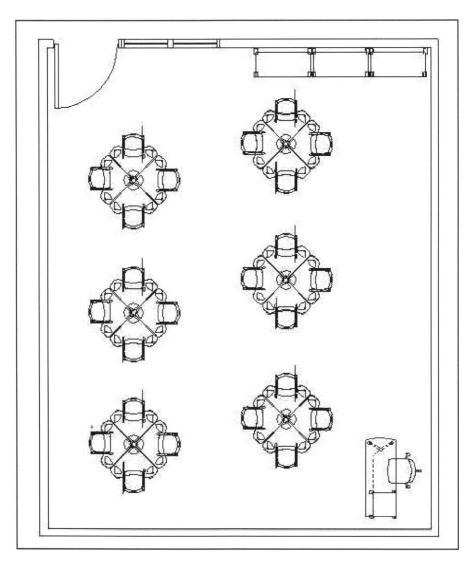

Collaborative Layout with desks in groups of four.

Collaborative Layout with desks in groups of four.

A variation on the Collaborative Layout uses pairs of **2-person desks** to make groups of four.

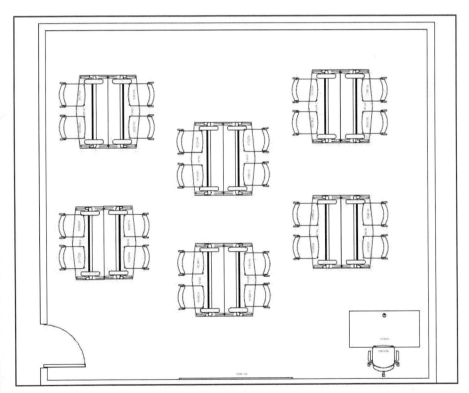

Collaborative Layout with pairs of 2-person desks.

Collaborative Layout with pairs of 2-person desks.

Another use of the 2-person desks allows for large group configurations like this rectangle layout that yields space for 24 students in sets of three 2-person desks on a side.

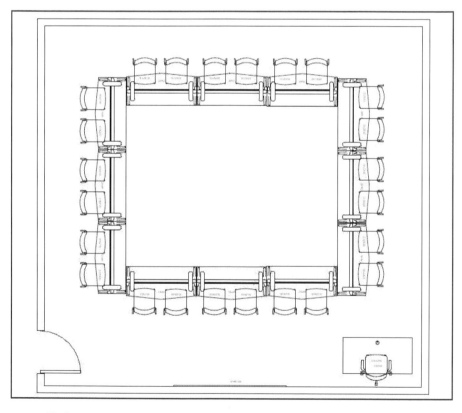

Collaborative Rectangle with twelve 2-person desks.

Collaborative Rectangle with twelve 2-person desks.

Collaborative settings can also be accomplished by the use of **tables** instead of individual student desks. Tables can come in a variety of shapes as well and can be configured together to make bigger groups or separated out for smaller groups or individual use. By adding casters to tables, it makes it much easier to move and reconfigure them within the space.

There are also tables that can flip up, called **flipping or nesting tables,** that allow the tables to easily be pushed out of the way, taking up far less floor space when not in use. This is ideal if the room needs to be cleared for other activities.

Flip-top tables

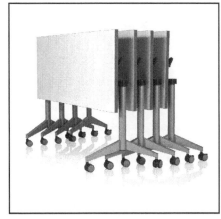

Tables shown "nested"

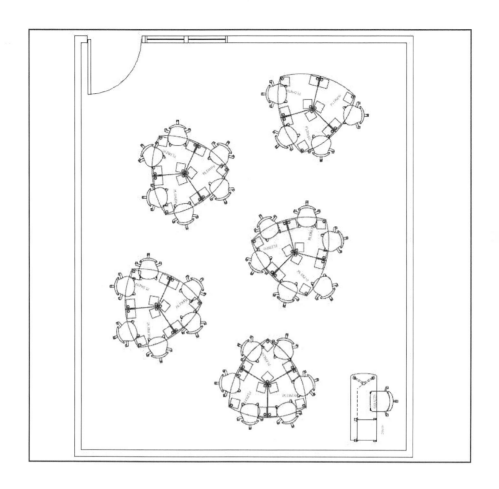

Collaborative Layout showing Shaped Tables.

4. ULTIMATE FLEXIBILITY LAYOUTS

The Ultimate Flexibility concept originated around 2010 with the introduction of new products into the market place. Manufacturers studied the use of classrooms and made discoveries that resulted in a new option for schools. This concept emphasizes the idea that movement helps facilitate a more flexible and collaborative environment.

For the first time, the students have everything they need in one piece of furniture coupled with the ability to move. The seats swivel, so now the student can adjust their attention to different material or to the person speaking. This allows all four walls to now come into play and removes the front of the classroom that has been the norm. Students can quickly move from lecture mode, to discussion mode, to group work, to testing mode - all in a matter of seconds.

When someone mentions the idea of collaboration and communication, the seats that swivel with the work surface attached now allows the students to make eye contact with each other. In the past, they may have to turn their bodies to try to look over their shoulder. The students also have storage options underneath the seats so they have all of their school materials and personal belongings with them as the room is re-configured.

Most people see the many upsides of using the Ultimate Flexibility configuration. From our research, here are some of the issues and how they were addressed.

1. ***The rooms look messy.*** For an educator that is used to clean, straight rows, this can be distracting. Additionally, custodians have had issues adjusting to how to clean the rooms because they were used to cleaning floors between the aisles.

2. ***Too much movement.*** Again, this issue seems to lie with the educator, not the student. The constant rolling and swiveling can cause anxiety to some teachers. For the students, the blatant movement due to the new idea that they do not have sit still all the time does tend to wear off within a few days.

3. ***Lack of worksurface space.*** Some subjects require a large work top area and due to the movement and engineering requirements, the worksurfaces are just not large enough. Most of the models on the market have a work surface large enough for a device and an 8 ½" x 11" paper or notebook.

To overcome these limitations, professional development is utilized to acquire new teaching skills on how best to use this type of furniture. In the history of classroom furniture, nothing has changed the learning environment as dramatically as this category of furniture. It immediately changes the classroom and the opportunities to learn differently. This type of furniture is best for 4th grade up to adult education.

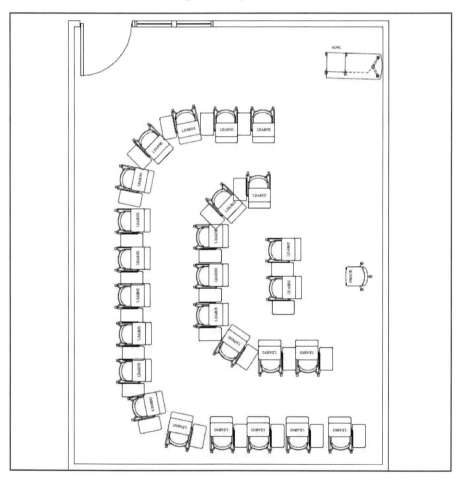

Ultimate Flexibility Layout in audience group setting.

Two 3D views of Ultimate Flexibility Layout at left.

The Ultimate Flexibility layout mobile chair/desk units adapt quickly to many configurations - whole group, small group, rows, and even individual breakout possibilities.

Whether teachers are lecturing, mentoring, testing, or adapting configurations to all these student activities, the choices are all available with mobile chair/desks.

On the following page an Ultimate Flexibility Layout is shown featuring groups of desks with both 4 and 5 students in clusters.

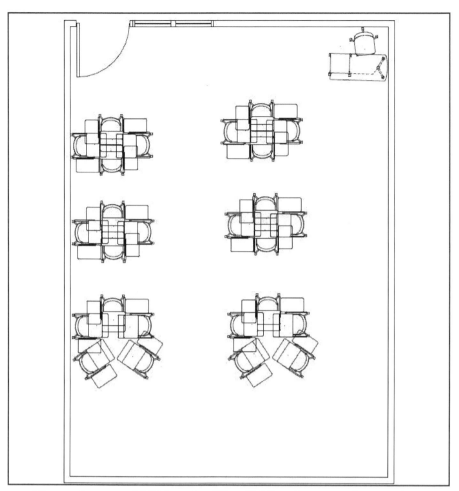

Two views of Ultimate Flexibility Layout featuring desks in groups of four and five students.

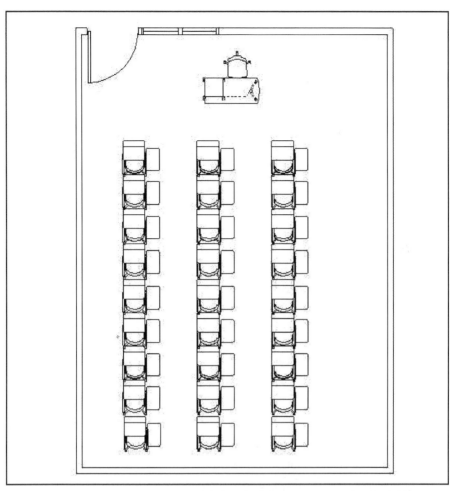

Two views of Ultimate Flexibility Layout featuring a more traditional lecture or testing configuration.

5. Team Based Learning Layouts

Team Based Learning is designing a classroom with the idea that the majority of the classroom time is spent in group work. Utilized in Project Based Learning environments, this arrangement is meant to allow the teacher to freely move throughout the room to engage in small groups. The groups of students have a more private space to work as a team. Many times, mobile room partitions can provide sound and visual barriers to separate groups. We have also advocated for many schools to use mobile marker boards for the same functionality, plus providing a visual work surface for the group.

The integration of 1-1 technology also provides many benefits in this classroom. A larger monitor in each group can be used to share one person's screen at a time. This allows the group to be working off the same screen instead of everyone huddling around one device. It also allows the teacher to share his or her screen to show the entire class. These larger monitors can be mounted to the wall or on a mobile monitor cart, giving the potential to re-arrange the classroom easier.

**Two views of Team-Based Learning Layout
in group configurations of pairs of 2-person desks.**

6. STUDENT CHOICE LAYOUTS

Student Choice is a philosophy that gives the student the ability to pick his individually preferred learning style. This layout is also referred to as Flex Seating in recent years. The variety of options and the removal of the assigned seats protocol in this arrangement changes the student mentality. This reinforces the mentality that students are in charge of their own spaces and learning goals.

When the students can pick what is most comfortable for them, they have a tendency to choose based on their predominant learning style. If they need to be active, they may pick a chair that allows movement or stand at a standing height table.

If they need a more relaxed environment for individual study, they will pick a lounge chair with a tablet arm to do their work, sit in a low bean bag chair, or even on the group. If they need the social aspect to talk through their ideas, they will sit in a booth or a table to facilitate discussion. The teacher typically will move throughout the classroom and be able to connect with students at each distinct area.

These rooms tend to be popular beyond the class period for staff meetings, parent events, and community use. In an era of student centered learning and personalization, the Student Choice concept is gaining popularity, especially for elementary aged students K-5.

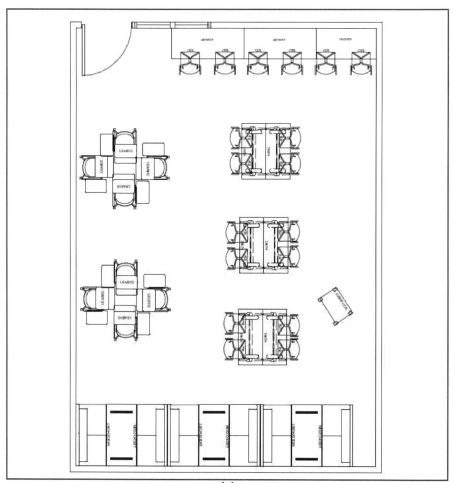

Two views of Student Choice Layout at left.

Summary

Choosing the right concept is essential before moving to the next step of this process. These 6 concepts are by no means the only ones available, but they are a good starting point.

There will be times that you want to explore a specific furniture item because of the way it looks, but you remember to revert back to your planning process and remind you why you selected a certain concept. To help you plan and add notes to each concept, download our website's free Planning Guide **www.kay-twelve.com/bookplanningguide**.

PART THREE

BUILDING A TEAM

Building A Team

If you are convinced that your current situation needs to be changed to provide a better learning environment, this section will help you take the initial steps to make it happen.

Every school or classroom design project starts with one person making the decision that something needs to change for the good of their students. This one person could be an administrator, teacher, parent, or even a student.

We refer to this person as The Champion. That "Champion" takes action to find other advocates and team members, internally and externally to get the knowledge and resources to make the plan a reality.

Finding an outside resource such as an architect, interior designer, space planning consultant, or furniture company can help facilitate the process and bring their experience and expertise on board. Some will do this for no cost; others will charge hourly fees.

There are many advantages to starting with a small project and focusing on one space. This will gain the interest of others and start making an impact right away. In some instances, if the project or space doesn't have a major impact on others, it may only require The Champion to convince one or two people to get approval to move forward.

Many teachers take on their classrooms themselves to make changes for their students' learning needs. This is commonly done by searching the web or Pinterest for ideas and then taking action. It is not uncommon for teachers to spend their own money or use annual stipends to fund any new furniture.

We are also seeing many teachers request financial assistance in many forms:

• Asking Administration for Funding

• Asking the PTO/PTA/HSA for Funding

• Asking Parents for Support

• Seeking available Grants at a state, regional or federal level

• Public Fundraising via *GoFundMe.com* or *DonorsChoice.org*

Although funding is typically considered one of the biggest challenges in preventing learning environments from evolving, it is typically poor planning as the main culprit.

We've witnessed many incidents where teachers try to take a project on alone. They jump to the conclusions of what furniture they need without adequately addressing the remaining steps in the process, such as building the support, before requesting funds. The funding request gets rejected and the teacher also feels rejected.

We advocate thinking through the whole process versus seeing something "cool" and charging ahead to find the money to make it happen. We have seen this team-building approach have much higher rates of success.

Envisioning The Future

The goal is to create a realistic scope with ideal outcomes, identifying obstacles, purchasing options (such as grants, donors, internal funding, etc.) and a time frame.

Once a clear Champion has emerged, the next step is developing a method to strategically plan for the best expected outcome. Depending on the scope of the initial project, this may result in a committee or core group of influencers.

The idea of a committee can sometimes be viewed as negative and daunting for valid reasons. It can be time consuming and frustrating to get many contrasting opinions. The Champion should make the decision on whether he or she wants to have a committee, or will just take the lead and consult influencers to build support for this process.

Whether you decide to assemble a committee or take the responsibility to just make it happen, here is a list of potential representatives:

- **Teacher(s)** interested in changing their space.

- **Technology Directors** and **Curriculum Directors.**

- **Parent(s) of a student** – Typically a PTA/PTO/HSA member would be a good choice.

- **Student(s)** – You can make it a reward system or include a class or group as part of this process (*See the Plainfield High School and The Linsly School case studies later in this chapter*).

• **Community Leaders** – These are your outside evangelists such as local government officials and business leaders. Great ideas can come from these people who will think outside the walls of the school, bringing up ideas you may have not considered, and suggesting potential funding sources.

- **School Board Members**
- **Local Government Representatives**
- **Chamber of Commerce, Rotary or Local Business Leaders**

SETTING GOALS

The next step is clearly defining the goal of the project. The Champion should be the one driving the intended outcome.

Here is a list of outcome examples we've seen:

- *Improved student engagement*
- *Shifted space to better accommodate technology*
- *Created a flexible space that can be easily re-arranged for multiple uses*
- *Designed a space that fosters collaboration*

Following the **SMART** goal setting example, the outcome should be **Specific**, **Measurable**, **Assignable**, **Realistic**, and have a **Timetable** or deadline.

SPECIFIC

Have a clear goal for your project be able to clearly communicate it. Keep asking the question "Why?" to make sure you are truly getting to the root of the problem you are trying to solve.

A good way to come up with this is to envision about how to describe the space a year after it has been implemented. *For example:*

Our new space has our students much more engaged than before. They come into class and choose where they are going to start the class. They have the freedom to pick from standing height desks, stools, standard chairs, comfy chairs, or areas on the rug.

They love that movement is the expectation. They are not confined to their previous desk and chair when they had to get permission to leave their seat. There are areas in the classroom where they can sit in groups for projects and also space when they need to focus on individual work or testing.

Parents give positive feedback because their children are talking about how this space is different than what they were used to in school. The space gets utilized after school hours because adults also like the flexibility and variety of options, including staff meetings, PTA/PTO meetings, and other community events. Due to the technology and class arrangement, there is no longer a front or back of the classroom.

The technology is easy to use and the teacher now has four monitors positioned throughout the room instead of a bigger one at the front of the room. The students can see the material better and the teacher can switch what is on each monitor or let the students share their screen to show the whole class or for project work. This classroom truly is a game changer in the way our teacher teaches and our students learn.

Once the vision is written out, a clear goal can be taken from key elements.

Here is an example of this vision put into a simple form:

We are striving to create a collaborative and flexible space that will allow us to use technology better and help our students become more engaged.

MEASURABLE

To make this measurable, the best way to begin is to have a baseline survey. Again, the amount of time and detail that goes into this should match the scope of the project. If you are starting with one classroom or a section of a classroom, asking for some feedback from students, parents, and other teachers may be adequate.

For a larger scope, circulating a formal survey may be more effective. Here is an example list of questions to ask using a free survey service such as www.surveymonkey.com:

Example Survey

We are in the process of re-examining our learning environments to better accommodate each style of learning. Please answer these questions honestly so we can make well educated decisions for our school.

1. On a scale of 1 to 10 (1 being lowest, 10 being highest), how would you currently rate the ability to see the teacher's presentation material.

2. On a scale of 1 to 10 (1 being lowest, 10 being highest), how would you currently rate the ability to hear the teacher when she is speaking to others.

3. On a scale of 1 to 10 (1 being lowest, 10 being highest), how would you currently rate your current comfort with your chair and desk.

4. On a scale of 1 to 10 (1 being lowest, 10 being highest), how would you currently rate your ability to move throughout the room when needed.

5. On a scale of 1 to 10 (1 being lowest, 10 being highest), how would you currently rate your ability to work in groups.

This survey can easily be modified to the intended recipients such as students, teachers, parents or administrators.

Some schools have utilized other metrics to try to measure student engagement. The Wellington School in Columbus, Ohio, developed a quick dot survey for their students. Throughout the day, students are asked to place an electronic dot on a graph to show their engagement. Those dots are then used as data points to show trends and feedback on student engagement.

CASE STUDY ON STUDENT ENGAGEMENT

THE WELLINGTON SCHOOL

COLUMBUS, OHIO

The Wellington School was seeking a way to measure student engagement, not rely on high-stakes standardized tests as the primary measurement of success. The challenge was to get simple and honest data from students that would give the administration accurate & actionable information

The basic premise of the tool was that Love of Learning equals Student Engagement. By creating an XY axis graph, they asked the students to place a dot on whether they were Challenged/Unchallenged and Hate It/Love It. Three times a year, each student plotted a dot for each class.

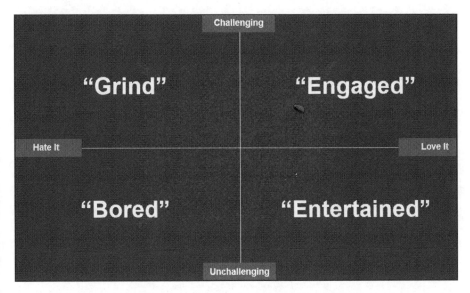

These data points were kept confidential by individual, with only administration access to student identity. With the collected data, clear trends were shown based on each quadrant.

If the student was Challenged and Loved It, they fell into the **Engaged** category, which meant they would most likely pursue more knowledge on the subject. If they Loved It, but were unchallenged, this resulted in an **Entertained** category. Hate It/Challenged was put in a **Grind** category and the Hate It/Unchallenged resulted in **Bored** students.

The key findings also helped the Head of School, Rob Brisk, use real-time data to help teachers identify areas of improvement. The teachers and parents never were shown individual student's information to keep the integrity of the data. The data was searchable by subject, teacher, and student. This live data is important, actionable information. Teachers can make adjustments and students may be able to be saved before it is too late.

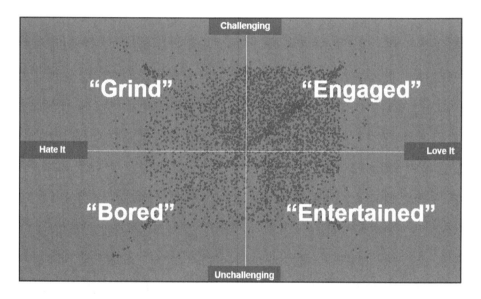

This graph shows all the students in aggregate of the teacher.

Initial Findings from Student Engagement Data

1. Connection to teacher
2. Mobility is important
3. Student autonomy is a great contributor to engagement

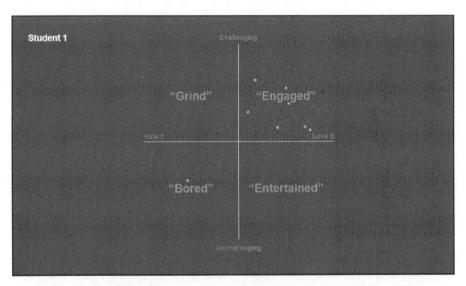

This graph shows the same subject comparing two teachers.

This graph showsan individual student throughout the day.

A follow up project to the Wellington Engagement Index was applying a wordle diagram to each quadrant. See the next page for two charts showing the frequency of words used to describe the "Engaged" quadrant and the "Bored" quadrant.

55

Wordle Diagram of words used to describe Engaged.

Wordle Diagram of words used to describe Bored.

There are future applications that Wellington foresees opportunities to use the WEI and other schools are now utilizing this tool in various areas, including as a factor in teacher evaluations. One of the surprises of this survey was that Brisk has yet to run into a teacher that thinks this data is irrelevant. This solidifies his trust in the data to make impactful decisions.

SET A TARGET

When deciding what you want to measure, it is also important to set a target.

Examples:

The space will improve student engagement by 25%

The space will improve student attendance by 10%

The space will improve overall happiness by 25%

The space will improve student (or teacher) retention by 20%

The space will help improve our conversion rate of student enrollments : school tours by 20%

Knowing specifically what you are trying to accomplish is similar to the concept of return on investment (ROI). It is always beneficial to be able to make a financial case for spending money. If you can clearly show that an investment brings in more return, it improves the likelihood of the project getting approval.

ASSIGNABLE

This means that someone owns a task or result. Take the approach that only one person can "own" a task. They may need help from others, but it is important that only one person has the lead and is ultimately accountable to get it done.

Examples:

Mrs. Jones, Principal, is leading the initiative to implement a 21st Century Classroom.

Mr. Thomas, 6th Grade English teacher is responsible to create a survey and get 20 responses.

REALISTIC

This is a mental check to make sure that the goal is not too daunting to be completed. Some leaders may ask others to reach a little further than their comfort zone, but everyone involved should feel like it is realistic to achieve. Continue to get feedback from others to see if there are concerns with the project in regards to scope, resources, and time.

Pick a time frame and stick to it. If the goal is to have something implemented by the beginning of the next school year, start with that and build milestones to the current date. From our experience, most schools are surprised how long the entire process can last.

Here is a realistic timeframe for most of our projects, starting with the end date in mind:

August 15th - Students return to school

August 8th - Classrooms are ready

July 31st - Space completed for teachers to move into classrooms

April 30th – Place order for furniture and materials. Our perception of ordering has changed in the Amazon era of Prime 2-Day Delivery. Many educational furniture manufacturers are very seasonal and do not start making the product until the order is placed. Due to demand for summer deliveries, lead times may extend to 12 weeks. This seems like a long time, but it will allow you to pick from a variety of colors and fabrics. Visit *www.kay-twelve.com/bookplanningguide* for a downloadable planning guide and more details.

April 15th – Select furniture options such as colors and fabrics.

March 31st – Selection of furniture items to be ordered.

March 15th – Final selection of layout after revisions.

February 28th – Initial layout to gain feedback for revisions.

January 31st – Complete **SMART** Goals

By combining all the aspects of SMART, here is a good example of a complete SMART goal:

Mrs. Smith is leading the initiative to implement a prototype active learning classroom that accommodates all learning styles by the beginning of fall semester that will increase student engagement by 10%.

Case Study on Student Involvement
Plainfield Community School Corp.
Digital Learning Grant
"Changing Learning Spaces at PHS"
Plainfield High School
Indianapolis, Indiana

Our Goals

#1 To provide continued support for our teachers with professional development to improve instruction from Level 1 to Level 4 in the SAMR Model.

Level 1 – Substitution – Computer Technology is used to perform the same task as was done before the use of computers.

Level 2 – Augmentation – Computer Technolog offers an effective tool to perform common tasks.

Level 3 – Modification – This is the first step over the line between enhancing the traditional goings-on of the classroom and transforming the classroom Common classroom tasks are being accomplished through the use of Computer Technology.

Level 4 – Redefinition – Computer Technology allows for new tasks that were previously inconceivable.

#2 To provide high quality Learning Spaces that promotes mastery of 21st Century Skills such as Teamwork, Collaboration, Critical Thinking and Creativity

CHALLENGES

1. **Financial Constraints**
2. **Teacher/Staff Buy In**
3. **Physical Constraints**

STAKEHOLDER INVOLVEMENT

- Plainfield High School Technology Steering Committee was established

- PD focused on curation of digital curriculum, student engagement and differentiation

- Community Forums were held to keep ALL stakeholders up-to-date on our 1:1 initiative

- Student input on device selection and project design was utilized

**Plainfield High School
"Before" pictures**

"Our Finding for Change – A Mindset Shift"

If your schools are filled with "teaching spaces" instead of "learning spaces," what are YOU doing to change that?

- Ira David Socol
Educational Technology & Innovation Team Leader
Grand Rapids, Michigan

"Classroom designs are moving away from a focus on the front of the room (and the instructor). In some cases student sit closer to the instructor or at small tables such as star clusters or circular tables. Small group conversations are encouraged, which improve learning."

- Creating multiple focal points in classrooms

- Grouping or clustering students rather than seating them in rows

- Establishing informal group work spaces

- Providing movable furniture

- Building reconfigurable spaces

<u>Learning Spaces</u>
by Diana G. Oblinge

**Plainfield
High School
Media Center
"After" Picture**

**Plainfield
High School
Media Center
"After" Pictures**

**Plainfield
High School
New Learning
Spaces**

SUMMARY

- *Roadblocks – None*

- *Project finished on time and under budget*

- *All goals were achieved*

- *Lessons Learned – The process cannot be rushed. Take your time and do it right the first time!*

Case Study on Student Involvement

Mrs. Allison's Comments

8th Grade Classroom Redesign Project

The Linsly School

Wheeling, West Virginia

2015 - 2016

Students used the stages of Design Thinking to redesign Classroom 213 at The Linsly School.

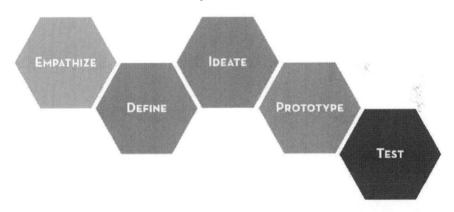

The Classroom Redesign project was inspired by 2 factors. I had attended a conference the summer before in Boulder, CO, on Design Thinking. In an effort to use this new instructional approach, I began to brainstorm ideas that I could implement in my own classroom.

Since I was beginning a new position as MS Dean, I was simultaneously thinking about a new configuration of my room. It seemed logical to offer this as a problem for my students to solve.

After reading several articles such as the one from Edutopia entitled *"Flexible Seating and Student-Centered Classroom*

Redesign" by Kayla Delzer, I decided to propose to my headmaster the idea for the Classroom Redesign project. He gave me the go ahead and promised to fund the winning student design.

DEFINING THE PROBLEM

The 8th graders in Mrs. Allison's classes worked collaboratively to conduct interviews with users of the classroom: teacher, students, and advisees.

From there, each class defined the problem: The classroom space of Room 213 serves as both a classroom and an administrative office. Each class defined the problem slightly differently, but most all recognized the following problems with the current design:

> • The space is not conducive for a discussion-based instructional approach, which requires student collaboration and effective student-to-student & student-to-teacher communication.

> • The space is not suitable for meetings of an administrative nature such as with parents and teachers.

> • The space did not allow for comfortable seating for advisees and for storage of advisee bookbags, sports equipment, etc.

See wide view picture below and additional views on facing page of Room 213.

Room 213

Design Process

- Each class divided into committees to create a written proposal, an itemized budget, and a visual design

- The top design from each class was presented to our Headmaster, Mr. Zimmerman, our Director of Facilities, Mr. Dodd, and a panel of judges. Students used a multi-media format for their projects and we conducted the formal presentations in the our school's 90-person capacity, multi-media classroom.

- The winning design, period 6, will be funded.

Timeline Challenges

The classroom redesign project was set to be carried out over the course of the 2015-2016 school year. We had hoped to have the student designs completed in the first quarter, but that didn't happen. Classes were given 1 hour per week to work on the project, but they needed more time (everyone's greatest resource!). We extended the student design deadline and the formal presentations were made in November of 2015.

Funding Challenges

Seeking funding for the actual redesign has been another challenge. Mr. Zimmerman has taken on that responsibility as he was the one who initially gave the go-ahead for the project. Unfortunately the funding was not secured before the end of the 2015-16 school year. This proved to be disappointing to the 8th graders who had become so engaged in the project, they were highly motivated to see it come to fruition.

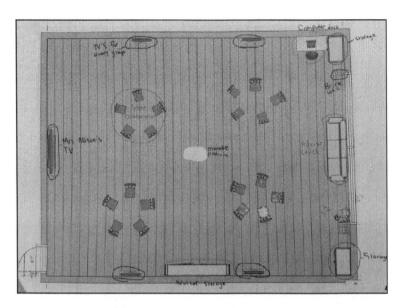

Here is the digital sketch of the winning design.

**And here are the winning students
(8th graders in period 6)**

PART FOUR

COLLABORATION

Choosing a Professional

At this point, if you haven't been working with an experienced professional, you will want to find a trusted partner that can help you with your project. This can range from an architect, interior designer, school furniture dealer, technology company, or consultant. Most likely, you will need to get input from a variety of these professionals.

Experience has proven to me that individuals who choose to work in the education market have a genuine interest in helping schools improve. It is important for you to verify this when you are seeking partners. To evaluate who to work with, understand the structure of each role and the best way for you to proceed. Also take into account the culture of the company and its commitment to the educational process.

Architect

An architect can help with conceptual drawings and any building modifications. Some architecture firms specialize in education and can bring an abundance of knowledge to assist in the process. The fee structures vary, but for smaller projects there will be an hourly rate with a "not to exceed" cap on price. If the scope of the project is clear and the firm has prior experience, they may offer a set fee structure. If the project is larger in scope, the fee structure typically becomes a percentage of the total cost of the project. Most architecture firms will have an interior designer on staff or have a recommendation for designers to hire.

Interior Designer

An interior designer will help you selecting products, colors, and fabrics. An experienced interior designer can also prepare specifications of items that will be used for bidding the items to be purchased. Do your research to see if the designer you select can match your vision of functionality with aesthetics. We've seen many schools listen to recommendations of interior designers to use custom colors and fabrics. When it comes time to add small quantities in the future or replace items, the costs are higher than expected, or may simply not be available in a smaller quantity. Providing clear direction of what you would like helps ensure that the right products and finishes are selected.

Furniture Dealer

Furniture Dealers can be a great resource for you since they have experience working with similar clients. Dealers usually have a specialty or focus on certain markets, such as corporate, education, or healthcare.

It is important to find a company that specifically works in the education sector. They will be more familiar with the trends, research, and typical budget constraints within a school.

An educational furniture dealer can be your best partner for projects that do not require an architect. For example, our company, **Kay-Twelve.com**, will help guide through this process to focus on the educational goals, figure out the best concept, and then provide several furniture options that match your cost range.

Some furniture dealers have interior designers on staff, but not all. Make sure you ask, because having drawings and high-quality 3D renderings helps visualize the space and build support for your project. Typically, furniture dealers do not charge for their in-house design services. Instead, they earn their fees from selling products.

Furniture dealers can also provide samples of the furniture so you can see it, touch it, and get feedback from the students and teachers. This partnership should be viewed as a long-term relationship that will be on-site to make your vision a reality. Timeframes are usually tight because most schools want the furniture delivered before school starts in the fall. A good partner will go above and beyond to make this happen and be responsive to any issues once the furniture is in use.

Technology Provider

Similar to the furniture dealers, technology providers charge fees on their products and services they perform. They will do an initial assessment at no cost to provide you with available options. A company that focuses on education will also be able to show you what other schools have done, be aware of the latest technology, and be a good partner throughout installation and on-going training and support.

CONSULTANT/OWNER'S REPRESENTATIVE

You may be able to find an experienced consultant that will walk you through this process and be your advocate. They typically work on an hourly rate or fixed price structure.

There are many retired educators that enjoyed going through this process in their prior role and want to offer their experience to other schools. Consider the consultant's experience and process to see if it is the right fit for you. We've seen consultants accelerate the process and save the schools considerable amount of money.

We've also seen consultants get in the way and let their agenda drive the project. If you are confident in your abilities and time available to do your own research and contact other professionals when needed, than a consultant may not be needed. Most of the time, the consultant is worth the investment.

COLLABORATION:

CREATIVE VS. TIME-CONSUMING

The collaboration stage is typically the most fun and creative phase. It can also be time consuming and daunting. Be clear with whomever you work with on both your budget and timeframe. There are so many products available on the market, all requiring different lead times in manufacturing, which is why we firmly believe you need to start well in advance of your deadline.

Establish your desired learning outcomes and choose a concept that would meet the objectives you want to achieve. There can be many revisions, so don't be frustrated. Take the time to get the concept right before focusing on specific furniture items.

Choosing the Right Products

For the most important items, ask to see samples or do a site visit at another school using them. An evaluation period can give you time to do your homework and gain feedback from those you defined in your process. This may include teachers, administrators, students, parents, and community members.

Using a quick survey will help you quantify the data. Here are a few pointers:

• Make the survey questions **specific to functionality**. For example, "is the work surface large enough to accommodate your typical work?"

• Attempt to **get feedback independent of colors**. For example, "Disregarding the colors, do you like the look of the chair?" Color has a tremendous impact on attitudes toward furniture. People make immediate emotional decisions based on the color of the furniture sample. It is important to try to separate the feelings of the color with the rest of the evaluation, since most furniture has many color options.

• **Data is important, but should not override the existing goals**. We've seen examples of schools that put in the early work and, because the ones being surveyed are not familiar with the concept you are striving for, the results came back in favor of the status quo. The product evaluation time is when you start hearing complaints and concerns from the ones that fear change.

For example:

If the furniture has casters (wheels), you may hear that the students will be all over the place, be disruptive, or even abuse the furniture. Our experience is that the newness of the furniture is short lived. After a week or so, the students adjust to the new environment. It is usually the teachers that have a harder time. We'll discuss professional development in the next chapter on implementation.

• Commit some time in doing research or seeking advice on the quality of the products. Warranties are extremely important on the product that you are choosing. Cheaper quality products can break down and create ongoing problems. You can avoid many issues by investing time on the front of the project.

Other factors that may contribute to selecting the right products:

• **Manufacturing Location** Is it imported or domestic and what matters to you? Imported products may have longer lead times, especially if they are not standard items.

• **Warranty Info** Most items for a school should have at least a 10-year warranty.

• **Certifications** BIFMA tested, Greenguard Compliant, and Global Educator Institute certified

• **Lead Times** Depending on how soon you need it, some products are available in less than 2 weeks and others can be 10-12 weeks. This is important not only for your first order, but when it is time for additional furniture or replacement items.

CHOOSING THE RIGHT FINISHES

The selections of color, materials, and fabrics is referred to as the finishes. This process is primarily opinion driven. Know that there is rarely a consensus and someone's opinion will ultimately prevail while others are rejected.

This is where a professional eye or consultant can make the recommendations and take on some ownership of the decision. We've seen schools make decisions to incorporate school colors and other schools make decisions based on color-based research.

The Importance of Color in a Learning Environment

Color's impact is often overlooked, yet it is a powerful influence in our everyday lives, affecting everything we see and do. Color studies indicate that it plays a role in emotion, productivity, communication and learning, and is an important element to consider in any environment.

Use of color can ultimately influence an individual's working and studying. Color helps define a room's purpose whether it is for quiet study, teacher-led instruction, group collaboration or relaxation.

The use of color can be broad, such as a room's wall color, or a select accent, such as chairs or tables, depending on the intended effect. Generally color use in schools has been limited to a neutral wall color with the school's colors added as an occasional accent.

There are many approaches to room and furniture color selection. One must look at the effects of color on emotion and relate that to the purpose of the learning space, guiding the color choices – on walls, on floors, and even on furniture.

Here are some practical guidelines for incorporating color into three different spaces in a school's interior, with a specific focus on furnishings.

The Classroom

Classrooms are used for a variety of purposes, but the main intent is active learning. For this reason, color in a classroom environment should maximize information retention and stimulate participation.

The key to creating an environment conducive to learning in a classroom is to not over-stimulate learners. Overstimulation is often caused by large amounts of bright colors, especially reds and oranges.

Calmness, relaxation, happiness and comfort are feelings elicited by colors such as green and blue. While it is best to have a calming and neutral color on the walls, furniture can add a splash of color to an otherwise dull classroom. Since color is not used in large amounts on furniture, it does not have the same effect as bright colors on walls.

• Select yellow furniture to elicit feelings of liveliness, energy, happiness and excitement.

• Red and orange in small quantities can also demand attention and attract learners' attention to detail – a great way to lead students to a certain part of the room for an engaging activity.

• If the intent is to match all elements of the room, use furniture colors that are similar to wall colors focusing on the calming greens and blues.

The one exception to color in the classroom is with younger children, who thrive in a bright-colored environment. In this instance, bright colors can be used on the walls and in the furniture. It can also be used to help children understand how certain areas of a room are used. For example, the blue chairs in the corner may be used as a reading and relaxation area, while the red table may be a free-play space.

LIBRARIES

Libraries are a multi-purpose, extended learning environment and require careful attention to color selection. Color in a library setting should be used to align emotions and behaviors with the purpose of the space.

Since different areas of a library are intended for different activities, have fun experimenting with color. Take a reading area, for example. As an extension of the learning environment, reading areas are intended to be calming and relaxing allowing learners to reflect. In this instance, matching calming wall colors – like greens and blues – with furniture colors maximizes the effects of color in this space.

In contrast, if an area is used for lounging and conversing, color can provide excitement. Consider using a more neutral wall color and experimenting with furniture color by using bright-colored cushions, fixed colors on lounging chairs or vibrant accents on table tops or shelving edges. Color selections might include deep reds, oranges and yellows, or pastels in any color combination.

COMMON AREAS

Entryways and cafeterias, are more informal and welcome conversation, excitement and play. The color choices in a common area are limitless, but still should reflect the purpose of the area.

The front entryway is usually the first space people see when they enter a building. Typical furniture can include bench seating or small tables conducive to last-minute studying or midday chats. As a common gathering place for students before school, after school and between classes, entry ways should welcome fun and conversation. The furniture should reflect this excitement through bold, energetic colors. The front entryway is often a good place to incorporate school colors into the furniture to welcome visitors with the school's spirit.

Cafeterias are also an area that allow for free time, and should also be energetic and welcoming. Feel free to use school colors on the walls, but use furniture to compliment. If school colors are bright, use furniture in similar tones. If the wall colors are muted or neutral, use bursts of colorful furniture to add life to the space.

GIVE COLORFUL FURNITURE A TRY

It is clear that color can have an effect on mood, emotion, and productivity, which ultimately influences student success. Let the purpose of the space guide the color scheme selection. With a little bit of thought and planning, adding color to any space can be easily accomplished.

Tips:

• If possible, select from standard options. This will keep costs lower, reduce lead times, and prevent costly additions in the future

• If you are using upholstered items, selecting the right material and Grade of textile is important. There is a wide range of quality and cost in textiles. In many cases, a vinyl type textile is chosen for the seat or the whole upholstered piece because of it's durability to handle stronger cleaning products such as bleach. Though that doesn't mean fabrics should be ruled out completely, as they often provide a variety of color and pattern to a furniture piece and space. Also, the types of cleaners that you can use should be documented.

• Before cleaning any upholstered piece, it's advisable to check what the cleaning code is for that textile, which can be found through the vendor of the textile. This will tell you what ratio of bleach (if at all) a textile can take, or if it can only be cleaned with a dry cleaner.

• If the furniture is in a high traffic area, select items that will last longer by evaluating the data. For example, looking at the number of double rubs a textile has undergone, can tell you if the textile is suitable for high traffic areas. However, this is not a hard fast rule, as tests going above the 100,000 double rub limit don't always show a indication of higher tolerance to abrasion, according to the Association for Contract Textiles (ACT). Spending time evaluating textiles in the project stage and the correct cleaning methods after installation, can ensure an improved life-span for your school's furniture.

CASE STUDY

TAKING A CONCEPT TO FINAL DRAWING

AND SPECIFICATION

EXAMPLE OF A SINGLE CLASSROOM

CHOOSING THE

ULTIMATE FLEXIBILITY LAYOUT

A school decided to take on one classroom as a test prior to making a commitment school-wide. The first one was a teacher that was asking administration to make the change. She did research on the web and read many articles about different classroom designs. Since she was teaching 7th & 8th grade English, she felt like the Ultimate Flexibility concept was the best fit for her. She wanted to create the best environment to foster discussion as a big group and also for small groups. After engaging the Kay-Twelve team, we were able to get measurements of the room, quantity of students, and create an initial layout seen below:

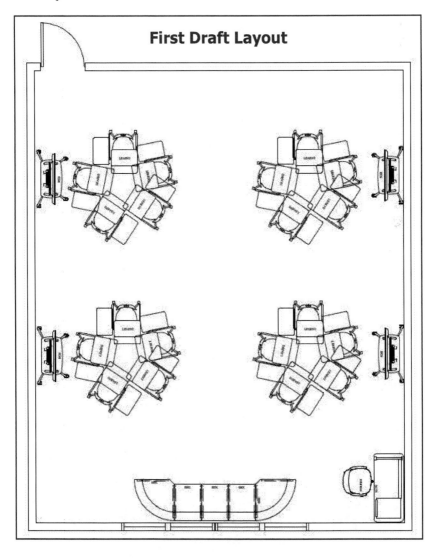

First Draft Layout

2D View of First Draft

Since the school was a 1-1 technology school, the concept of having mobile monitors would give the small groups an opportunity to work from a shared screen.

When the monitors were not in use, they could be moved out of the way or even shared with other classrooms or spaces throughout the school.

We included an area that allowed casual, soft seating for when students desired a different setting for discussion or individual study. Since the soft seating is modular, pieces can be separated or put together into a couch configuration.

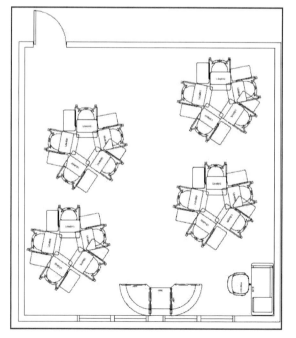

Final Draft Layout

After further discussion and examination of the budget, they decided to not have the mobile monitors at this time. They loved the idea of groups and that it could easily be reconfigured into discussion mode and testing mode.

We also needed to remove some of the modular soft seating to free up more space and budget. The teacher thought she may want to add the mobile monitors and add the soft seating down the road, but it would be better to start small and add if necessary.

At this point, we all agreed this was the best layout and started to discuss the actual products. For this concept, there were 4-5 products on the market that achieve the same goals.

We started with our suggestions and immediately trimmed it down to 2 products on aesthetics alone. The teacher requested to see samples of the remaining options, and this allowed the teacher and students to test them out and give feedback.

After this step, a clear winner had emerged. We then selected the colors and put together a final drawing and rendering with the color selections. This was the final piece that helped secure the funding for the project and get administration support. They shared the renderings with the staff and students, which created a buzz of excitement.

Final Draft in 3D view without the monitors and with some of the modular seating removed.

Part Five

Implementation

Implementation

The next step in the process is to focus on the timing and coordination of switching out the old furniture with the new.

Once all of the furniture and colors are selected, it is now time to place your orders. This process alone can take days to weeks, depending on your school's ordering procedures.

After the order is sent to the furniture dealer, it can take several days before the order information is confirmed by the factory. So keep in mind, the lead times that manufacturers are providing only start once the order is received by the factory.

Typically lead times can be 3-4 weeks during non-peak times, and up to 12 weeks in the summer months. While you are in this waiting period, there are many things that can help ensure a smooth transition.

One key issue that may arise with the implementation process is how you plan to dispose of the old furniture. Many schools try to retain still usable furniture and rotate out the worst. Other schools will try to sell or auction off their used furniture. Either way, having the spaces cleared out before the new furniture arrives is important, and requires more planning if done during the school year.

Stay in communication with the furniture dealer to try to coordinate the timing of this closely. They should be giving you periodic updates on the status. If you haven't heard from them, do not wait to look into the status at the last minute.

It is normal for new furniture to be shipped from the factory to a warehouse closer to your location. The items will be received at the warehouse and consolidated with the items coming from other locations. These are then loaded back to another truck for the final delivery to your school.

Many times this final stage requires a smaller truck to navigate better when there is limited access into a neighborhood school. Make sure the truck is equipped with a liftgate to assist unloading the furniture if the school does not have a loading dock.

Lastly, it is very important to clarify any obstacles that may hamper the delivery before the final quote is determined. Delivery obstacles may include; no elevator, limited elevator space, tight hallways and door frames, flooring that may not be able to handle heavy traffic.

All of these extra steps add days to the process and can be frustrating if it is not clearly communicated. We have all been spoiled in this Amazon age of two-day delivery right to your front door. Although manufacturers are getting better at predicting demand and stocking certain items, most school furniture items are still made-to-order.

Here are some common issues that occur during the implementation process:

COMMUNICATION & INSTALLATION ISSUES

• Are the items clearly marked for which room they will go in?

• Will stairs or an elevator be accessible?

• Are there enough people scheduled for delivery and assembly within your timeframe?

• Damage to the furniture. In this case, you and the installer should be taking many pictures. When and how the damage occurs has a significant impact on the resolution with regard to both time and money. Once you notice damage, make an immediate note of it, take pictures, and contact your furniture representative. Too many times we've seen when this step is delayed, later it becomes significantly harder to pinpoint who's responsible for the damage. These delays also expose you to being stuck with damaged product or paying for repairs or replacement.

• Lack of access during summer hours. School hours during the summer vary and the building is not always open. Plan ahead to make sure someone with a key and proper access is available.

PROFESSIONAL DEVELOPMENT

Some schools wait until the new furniture is installed and ready to go before considering professional development of the staff. This can lead to days or weeks of frustration and negative feelings about the new furniture.

In fact, properly preparing and training of the staff is one of the most critical success factors in this process. Take the time to schedule professional development sessions. These sessions should include:

- Perspective from other teachers that recently went through this transition

- Thorough discussion from the administration's point-of-view of why changes were made

- Clear expectations on how the new space will be utilized

- Other experts such as specialists, furniture representatives, or design staff

- Common issues during the implementation process, and how to avoid them

Follow up sessions should also be planned as the staff and students get acclimated beyond the initial transition period. There may be some staff that is initially resistant to this change and will need some assistance on how to change their teaching habits.

Introducing new concepts can be a real challenge. Some teachers struggle with the lack of uniformity and feel like the room is messy or unorganized. We encourage you not to dismiss this but rather engage to help the teacher modify habits.

Some students may also struggle, especially if the learning environment does not match their learning styles mentioned earlier in this book. So as a teacher is getting used to his new surroundings, he will also have to be reminded to carefully examine his students needs.

IMPROVEMENTS TAKE TIME

Acclimation is not immediate. Overall, this transition period may take weeks to months. This is also a time for trial and error. During this time period, we hear feedback that is both positive and negative, but in almost every instance they are surprised by something during the process. Like we mentioned in the introduction of the book, the decision to create a better learning environment is not meant to be a one time change. It is a process that requires continual progress and the experience of your partners that can add significant value during this phase.

CASE STUDY

LARGE URBAN HIGH SCHOOL

TEACHERS SHARING CLASSROOM SPACE ADOPT ULTIMATE FLEXIBILITY LAYOUT

This high school had a large classroom that is shared by two teachers. Some parts of the day the classes are combined and other times both teachers have their own class. They wanted to establish a flexible space with a variety of options for the students and the ability to have multiple group settings. The goal was to test many different options and gain feedback on how to proceed with future classrooms within the entire district.

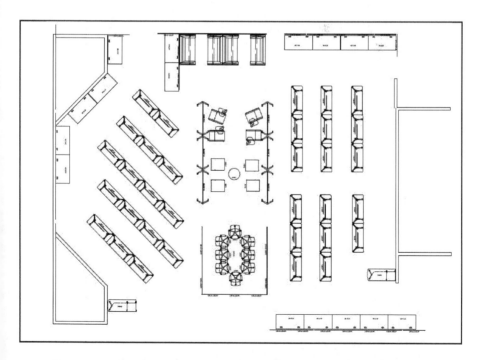

Layout of shared space with mobile dividers in center.

The plan to have mobile room dividers would allow them to create division between the classrooms when needed and also provide writable surfaces for student use. The mobile partitions could also create privacy areas for individual study.

They tested one side of the room using 2-student tables and the other side utilizing mobile student chairs with work surfaces. The student tables have individual marker boards that the students can use to show their work and display on an easel when presenting their information. When not in use, they can hang on the side of the table or be positioned as dividers to create privacy for testing needs.

Pictures after installation

Here is the actual feedback from the teacher after 3 months of use:

> We are still enjoying many of the attributes of the room and furniture. The quote board is coming along, we really enjoy using the whiteboard with the tables, and the standing desks are still a hit. However, if we were going to do it over, we'd probably change a few things.

90

First, the large conference area takes up too much space. We'd make it smaller and we'd face it toward the middle of the room, or as a sort of hallway divider. It's nice to be able to see into it, but the voices carry too easily, so it is not as separated as we'd imagined. Otherwise, we like having the storage space for us and the conference table for student groups.

Also, we'd rethink the desks. There is just too much movable furniture in the room. The students take advantage of the desks, and it makes assigned seating and neatness very difficult (even when the desks are "aligned," they look messy).

The kids really like the flexible seating with the desk arm side, but the surface is a little too small, flimsy, and very hard to clean. The tables, though they are big, provide flexibility because they can be moved if needed and the chairs are on wheels, so we think we'd keep the tables and get some more sturdy, non-wheeled desks. We still like having desks for students who need to spread out, need space, etc... just not on wheels.

We really like the dividers with the whiteboards. They especially proved invaluable for the many weeks when my Smartboard wasn't letting me write. I had to show content on the board, then pull over a whiteboard to use. We also like them as dividers and rolling content platforms. We have been doing splits almost every day, and they help to create a little buffer between the sides. We wish there were even a few more!

We like the new conference table, too, though it's a little tight inside it sometimes and really loud when the kids hit the sides with a chair. We don't really use the "material" aspect of the wall surfaces white board and posting space, but we could improve on this and the kids really like the work space. Most of our furniture concerns (the fact that everything moves) are because of the immaturity of our students. We think upperclassmen would use the materials a little better.

Breakout small group space between classrooms.

CASE STUDY

PRESENTATION SCHOOL

SONOMA, CALIFORNIA

TRACY WALTHARD, ASST. HEAD OF SCHOOL

DIRECTOR OF CURRICULUM

SUMMARY OF PROCESS:

The Presentation School began to look at the idea of new furniture during the 2015-16 school year. Our existing furniture was nearing its end of life, but more importantly, it impeded our ability to be flexible with our space and meet the needs of our student learners. Our board of trustees approved the annual Spring golf tournament in May 2016 to launch the fundraising campaign. During our Fall 2016 largest fundraiser, Imagine, the fund-a-need was Flexible Furniture, with a push to complete the fundraising of the needed $100,000.

Our school is a small private independent school located in Sonoma, CA, just north of San Francisco, nestled in the wine country. We have 185 students, one class per grade, a science lab, art studio, music room, and tech room.

Fundraising was left to the Head of School and Development office. However, a more challenging step to furniture adoption is faculty consensus, buy-in, and education. New furniture was the boards' idea, not the teachers. Although a good idea, we needed to begin working with the teachers to help them see that the money spent here would be equally or more valuable than new curriculum or other teacher priorities. The end of the year professional development for the 2015-16 school year included the launch of furniture vision casting and discussion. Faculty was then given recent scholarly articles to read over the summer vacation.

93

In the fall, teachers were invited to an after school symposium to explore the idea of applying design thinking to furniture adoption. Teachers were then challenged to consider the needs of the classroom from a teacher and student prospective, record their ideas, and even complete floor plans. DREAM BIG was the theme – we didn't want a sense of what is possible to limit our vision. In addition to voluntary teacher participation, several teachers brought the idea of, "What is needed in the ideal classroom to enhance student learning?" directly to the students. These ideas were collected and shared with administration.

Before our large fundraiser, in which we hoped to finalize funding for flexible furniture, we had a demo classroom set up in the 7th grade. It had various types and sizes of furniture. The 7th grade was able to spend a week learning in this classroom. An additional week had the 7th grade off site, so K-6, 8 signed up for slots and rotated through for teacher/student experience. The furniture was also present for the Imagine event. During the Fund-a-Need portion of the evening, we brought several pieces that "looked" innovative into the event and several students who spoke to their experience in the demo class, their favorite pieces, and how they felt it improved the learning environment. The Fund-a-Need was a success.

A month later, connected to Thanksgiving break, we had a day of PD to look again at flexible classrooms and diverse learners. We needed not only a classroom that could quickly adapt for instruction, but various seating options that allowed for individuals to seek the optimal seating for their learning style. As a single design of flexible seating it addresses one issue, but not the need for individualized learners. Keeping students "center" became a challenge during this time. It's not about what the teachers want and how new furniture will make teaching how they teach easier, it's about providing a new type of a learning environment that makes learning easier for the student!

During this time the faculty identified the three key needs in a classroom, whole class, group, and individual workspace.

**Installation
Photos**

**Installation
Photos**

We all agreed that the options should include the ability to quickly change between these three instructional methods.

Following the professional development, surveys were sent to all faculty and middle school students asking them for feedback on the demo room experience. These were compiled by students, K-2 faculty, 3-5 faculty, and 6-8 faculty, including specialized teachers to travel from room to room. From this information administration began looking at furniture option. Teachers were encouraged to add to the DREAM wall, where pictures were posted and faculty could leave notes for feedback.

The school then contracted with Kay-Twelve to help with renderings so we could look at school and layout. Multiple renderings for each grade were created and shared with divisions during Friday morning faculty meetings. Feedback from these sessions helped guide administration to narrow the choices. Working within budget, and a commitment to replace all student furniture in our classrooms, multiple options for each grade were presented to teachers by division.

Additional samples of furniture were ordered for demo. In March of 2017 a preliminary order was compiled and shared with faculty. Due to budget constraints, the faculty met to pare down the order. Outside picnic tables were removed as were new teacher desks. The teachers decided that student tables/desks and chairs that allowed for movement were the top priority. The final order reflected this.

After a draft order was completed, we had two parents, both designers, walk the school and give finish and color feedback. This was shared with the teachers, and selections solidified. When ordering, teachers in the lower school choose the edging on tables and the color of the sure edge. They chose the number of each type of seats for options. The faculty buy-in and understanding the purpose of new flexible movement furniture was key.

In the end, our teachers focused on the student's' ability to collaborate, but still have individual space. Every classroom has at least two desk/table seating options, with natural movement being the primary goal. All classrooms will have furniture on casters for quick arrangements from whole class, groups, and individual seating.

Our goal was to have furniture in classrooms by December 2016. We will have furniture on April 29th, 2017. Pushing the process to make the deadline would have compromised the quality of decisions and the outcome. By January, administration met and committed to a Spring Break install in March. We didn't make that either.

You need to stay focused on the end goal – quality furniture carefully picked to the met the needs of your students. *However, parents (who funded the project) and teachers still need frequent updates, so they know it is at least moving forward.*

Over the summer, faculty will read an admin chosen book (*The SPACE: A guide for educators*) about classroom design and furniture arrangement. During our beginning of the school year PD, teachers will implement new design elements into their classroom arrangement to reflect key learning from the reading. We will then do a gallery walk where each teacher will explain why they arranged their classrooms as they did, and how it reflects our summer reading.

Flexible furniture and furniture that allows for body movement is new. It's exciting. I look forward to hearing the teachers share in the upcoming year about the challenges, but mostly the successes experienced. They will be sharing out where they see improvement in student learning and engagement.

The process seems cumbersome. It is. But truly, the real work will begin once the furniture arrives. If teachers continue to use innovative flexible furniture in a fixed mindset, it's just furniture. It's the teacher's' design of the room, and instructional practices that will change the learning. The furniture should enhance their ability to move into new instructional practices. Furniture alone doesn't change education; only teachers do that.

Lessons Learned:

As an administrator, I wanted to finalize the project and make quick decisions. The educating of the faculty and creating buy-in is essential. Without it, the new furniture would be just furniture, with no real impact. By slowing down, helping teachers discover the current barriers to learning in their classrooms, brainstorm solutions, and be part of the selective process, they are ready not just for new furniture, but new instruction.

Part Six

Evaluate
& Communicate

Once the new furniture has been installed it is important to take stock of all the work that went into your project. There are many ways to ensure that all the time, effort, and money make a positive impact on the intended results.

We'll cover the primary areas that need to be addressed:

• **Take Pictures and Video.** The room will never look better than the first day of class. These pictures will come in handy for many purposes detailed below. Higher quality is better, but most phones today do a great job, so don't hesitate to take many pictures and videos from different angles, set up the room in different configurations, and try to include people in the photos if possible.

• **Professional Development.** Educators are no different from any other humans. They may struggle with change and resort to old habits. The primary complaint that we've seen is the acceptance of movement in the classroom. If the teacher is used to straight rows in the classroom, she may have problems keeping her concentration while students rock, swivel, or roll. This is a normal reaction and the result may be new rules to limit movement or trying to resort to the old configuration. Providing appropriate professional development and resources will help a teacher who is struggling with this change.

We worked with a school that tried the Ultimate Flexibility concept in four elementary classrooms. A few months into the school year, we sat down with all four teachers to get feedback. One teacher loved it, two teachers were getting used to it, and one teacher actively fought the changes and had daily battles with the students to keep it in the old configuration. At this point, the Principal had a few options. She could take the new furniture out and give it to another teacher or she could help the teacher see the benefits of the change and coach their teaching style around it.

• **Analyze.** Take the same measurement tactic used in the planning phase and use it to evaluate the new situation. Are the results positive or negative? What feedback was anticipated or unforeseen? Now, take that information to make future changes not only to the new space, but also for existing spaces. Can this information help in areas that did not receive new furniture? Can the data and feedback help the staff in other ways? It is always good to document this information for future use.

• **Internal Communications to Staff.** Send the information within the internal channels, whether it is email, newsletter, flyers, or social media. Others are interested in the outcomes and want to learn from their peers.

• **External Communications to Community.** Send information outside of the school. Everyone has a vested interest in the progress of schools. When preparing the message, make sure you are focusing on the right topics for the intended audience.

> • **Local Newspapers.** A resource that views all school news as relevant to their community, and is always seeking positive stories. Your pictures will add the visual element to their print stories.

> • **Local Publications.** Seek local newsletters from any of the surrounding neighborhoods. There is a growing trend for hyper-local publications that thrive on news about their neighbors.

• **Social Media**

> • **Facebook.** Share on the official school pages, but don't forget about the additional group pages that have major influences in the community. These include PTA pages, neighborhood pages, business community pages, etc.

• **Social Media** - *Continued*

> • **Twitter.** A brief way to get some clicks. Good to have a link going to another source with more information.

> • **YouTube.** Create a video showing the use throughout the day. This is a great student project. Laguna Beach Unified School District in California took this to a new level. In an engaging video that parodies the television show "The Office," students appear in the video to describe the difference between their traditional classrooms and the new 4C Learning Environment, they call it the **4CLE**. The results are highlighted and they piggyback it with a fundraising campaign to finance new classrooms. *https://www.youtube.com/watch?v=jRFElC2SR7E*

> • **Blog.** Schools blogs, individual blogs, and other educational sites are always seeking guest bloggers such as Edutopia.org or our own website **www.kay-twelve.com.**

> • **Pinterest.** Great way to share visual information.

• **Local Television** - Local TV, like local newspapers, find schools a constant source of interest. Additionally, most local news channels have many time slots to fill for morning, evening, and night broadcasts. A story about a school is usually not time-sensitive and can be used as a filler during slow news days.

• **Education Associations** - There are many associations specifically for education. If you are not a member of one, find those that are applicable and ask them if you can be part of a newsletter, or speak about your experience at an upcoming conference.

• **Partner with Partners** - The companies that helped you with this project also want to share the story. Reach out to them and see if there are creative ways to highlight your project. They may also have staff available to do this for you so it doesn't take much of your time. Your experience can live on as a case study in their presentations to other clients and on their websites.

• **School Tours** - Tours are used for many purposes. It can be for new parents and students visiting the school, community members, or prospective staff, just to name a few. Make sure to include your new spaces as part of the tour to highlight the improvements and focus on creating a better space to learn.

• **Promotional Videos** - Many schools produce videos as a way to communicate to prospective parents the benefits of the school. Here is a good example of Hillbrook School in Los Gatos, California. The Head of School, Mark Silver, explains what sets the school apart: *https://www.youtube.com/watch?v=uwDrnszy4lI*

Overall, sharing your story helps everyone in the education world. The more examples and resources that are available, the easier it is for future changes and improvements.

In the following pages we offer as a case study the architectural overview of a proposed addition to a large high school in Illinois.

Stevenson High School has consistently rated one of the top public high schools in America. The reputation is a combination of many aspects based on facts such as student test scores, graduation rates, and college placement.

However, the image of the school is something the leadership team focuses on to remain at the top of the list. *In a business sense, they have created a brand*. This brand allows them to continually improve and create more opportunities for their students. The leadership views each part of their facilities as part of this plan.

CASE STUDY

COMMUNICATING TO THE COMMUNITY

ADLAI E. STEVENSON HIGH SCHOOL

LINCOLNSHIRE, ILLINOIS

ARCHITECTURAL OVERVIEW FOR

PROPOSED BUILDING ADDITION

The following are highlights from an architectural overview power point entitled Adlai E. Stevenson High School – District 125, Village of Lincolnshire, Committee of the Whole – Final Presentation, East Building Addition, January 23, 2017.

The report begins with statistics showing the growth of the area's population and supporting the projected need for additional classroom space in the coming decade. It weighs the alternatives to building the proposed extension of their existing high school listing the advantages and disadvantages of a split schedule, mobile classrooms, and a link lab expansion with only 8-10 classrooms and high cost/space ratio.

Finally it shows the advantages of the new addition: 21 teaching spaces to accommodate the anticipated enrollment, no demolition, new spaces allowing for evolving delivery of instruction, Green roof with greenhouse teaching spaces, and Net Zero energy performance. The only drawback shown is the high construction cost.

By preparing this report, the school continues to get press attention such as an article with accompanying pictures in their local newspaper, The Daily Herald, entitled *"$28 million Stevenson Addition Aims to 'Reinvent the Classroom'"* **(and being highlighted in this book**).

This attention has financial significance by helping gain community support and attracting more families that want their children go to the best school.

106

As a result, ground breaking has already taken place in the summer of 2017. This cutting edge building addition assures the citizens of Lincolnshire that their high school will continue to accommodate their growing student population.

The 56,800 square foot three-floor addition includes classrooms, small group breakout rooms, science labs, a world language lab, multi-purpose rooms and storage. A fourth enclosed instructional level on the rooftop includes a greenhouse.

Between the two buildings is a carefully landscaped open space providing outdoor areas for lectures and instruction. Each floor of the addition is connected with corridors on each end to the existing East Building.

Architect's vision of the proposed addition to the East Building at Stevenson High School.

The roof features solar panels and several living green spaces with species native to savannah and prairie ecosystems. Farm crop plots that are ADA accessible and gardens offer many crossover classroom opportunities with the science, art and food and special education students.

The rooftop plantings will insulate the classrooms beneath reducing energy costs and combined with the solar panels bring savings and sustainability. The roof also houses a weather station.

Inside, the second and third floor corridors feature 2-story "living walls" with plants that enhance air quality and the environmental aesthetics of the open spaces.

Architect's vision of the First Floor corridor featuring breakout spaces for small groups.

Architect's vision of a Science Lab classroom with mobile stools and lab tables plus interactive screens.

Architect's vision of the Rooftop level.

Enclosed area includes a greenhouse and solar panels.

Even the two bridging segments of the addition
(*the long building at left*) connecting it to the existing
East Building (*the gray area at right*) feature
live planting on their roofs.

The open garden plots are mostly flat beds, though
some ADA accessible raised beds are provided.

Near the top of the illustration is the
semi-circular small class gathering spot.

In between the two buildings at ground level
is a lovely open courtyard landscaped
with walkways and seating for small classes.

On the wall of the addition that faces the courtyard
can be seen the "living wall" that is exposed
inside between the second and third floors inside.

Bonus Section

Part Seven

Shared
Learning Spaces

Shared Learning Spaces

Up until this point, we've used classrooms as the focal point to creating better learning environments. However, the use of other spaces throughout the school can have an equal impact on students' learning experience. There are several different areas and names for these types of spaces around the school. The idea is examine each area of your facilities - indoors and outdoors - and try to utilize those spaces for educational opportunities. There are many terms to describe these spaces such as **Collaboration Spaces**, **Makerspaces**, **Innovation Labs**, **Third Spaces**, **Collaboratories**, or **Flex Spaces**.

Library/Media Center/Learning Commons

Technology has been the main driver for converting traditional libraries into media centers. The decreased demand and need for physical books also provides more options for the space. Concepts such as benching systems, soft seating, and mobile partitions that create distinct learning areas have become increasingly popular.

Malvern Preparatory School in Pennsylvania recently engaged in a similar project. The traditional library was being utilized much less and they decided to clear out the entire space of the book stacks and wood tables. It immediately brightened up the space as the windows now became visible.

Head of School, Christian Talbot, explained that the new space was purposefully left open with the intention of creating a dynamic and and interactive place to inspire students to connect, collaborate, and create.

The layout at right shows the use of a variety of options and heights. The cluster of soft seating allows a few people to sit on each piece in a variety of positions. The high cafe tables and stools adds another dimension. The use of the stair seating is typically a popular place for casual sitting and discussion.

Cafeteria

These examples of cafeterias provide many different attributes that go beyond serving food. The cafeteria takes up a good portion of square footage in the facility and is being used throughout the day, not just during lunch hours. Community meetings are now in a comfortable setting. Staff can meet as a whole or in smaller groups.

We also see the cafeteria used as an alternative classroom when teachers need a change of setting or larger worksurfaces for certain lesson plans. The availability of monitors for multiple purposes can be utilized.

The key components for this "flex" space are chairs and tables with casters as well as using tables with nesting capabilities. This allows quick reconfigurability.

With the available options of high performance upholstery, it is realistic to add some soft seating and booth options that are easily cleaned and durable. Different height seating provides a variety of chair choices and less uniformity within the space.

Another important element is natural day lighting and being able to showcase large windows bringing in daylight and views which has proven to improve a student's performance and mood.

Photo Courtesy of Media Technologies

Photo Courtesy of Media Technologies

LOBBY

Many schools are creating lobbies to be more of a casual meeting and waiting area. Since this is the first impression of the school, many schools are re-thinking how to make lobbies a more inviting and useful space.

With the increased school choice options from public, charter, and private, the impressions you leave on the community and parents are vital. The lobby now functions as a recruiting tool.

Photo Courtesy of KI

Additionally, this space can be used for small group meetings and one-to-one interactions.

Using soft seating with sled bases allows components to be moved by students and adults without damaging the furniture or flooring. Having tables and power options welcomes the use of technology. The finishing touches of thoughtful lighting and plants create a comfortably inviting environment.

EXTENDED LEARNING AREAS

Outside the overall goal of creating effective learning spaces, there is the secondary goal of effectively utilizing all of the space with a school.

One example is re-examining the use of hallways and converting that space into **Extended Learning Areas** or **ELA's**. This example shows space for individual study, group work, or 1-on-1 student & instructor conversations that can take place outside of the classroom.

These spaces are typically in use while classes are in session as a quieter place to talk and concentrate. Before and after student school hours, these spaces become the hangout for staff, parents, and other community members.

It provides a casual, comfortable, and inviting feel that leaves a good impression of the school. The school now becomes a place that people want to be, especially for extracurricular events.

Huber Heights Middle School, Ohio

116

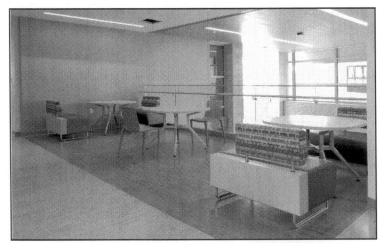

Photo Courtesy of KI

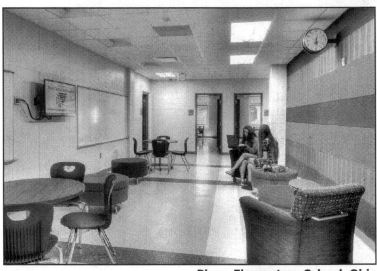

Piqua Elementary School, Ohio

MAKERSPACE, FAB LABS, IDEA LABS, COLLABORATORY, ETC.

The increased focus on doing and making for those tactile learners has sparked a trend in education toward **Makerspace** areas. These spaces have also been called **Collaboration Spaces, Idea Labs, Fab Labs, Collaboratories, Innovation Spaces** or **Flex Classrooms.** There are differences between some of these, but for the purposes of this book, we'll group them all together for now as non-traditional classroom spaces.

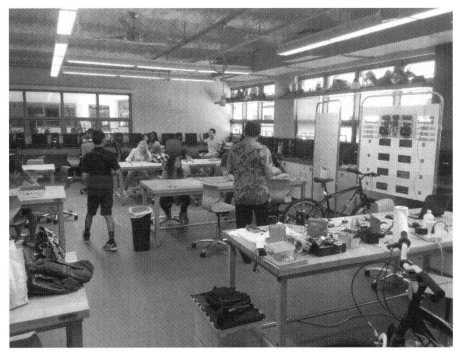

The Maker Space at Iolani School (2014)

Image via New York Hall of Science

CASE STUDY ON SHARED SPACES

CINCINNATI HILLS CHRISTIAN ACADEMY

HEAD OF SCHOOL, RANDY BRUNK

Randy creates a culture for his staff to not look at impediments, but to think of bumps in the road as roadblocks that they need to overcome.

Two problems exist with innovation in the classroom:

1. It's all on the teachers to make it happen and keep kids engaged. It is all on the teacher's shoulder to make it innovative.

2. A classroom is not really a great place for a lot of the things that need to be done because of the cultural context that students see as a place to focus on grades, following the rules, and raising your hand. Just by taking the kids outside of the classroom and into different spaces throughout the school, it changes the environment. They become more engaged, more focused, they aren't looking at their phones, or chit-chatting together.

As a leader, he needed to show the teachers that he was serious about creating engaged learning spaces. To do this, he raised money and allocated spaces for the teachers to use beyond the classroom. The Teacher Innovation Fund was proactively put in place so when the teachers had new ideas of things they wanted to try, the money was already available. This also took the weight off the teachers to do it in a traditional classroom environment, sending the message that it may not be you that is the problem, it may be the environment.

Some of the projects from the fund included Innovation Spaces beyond the primary classroom. Spaces that teachers can take their classes to as an alternate environment. They moved their administration offices to free up more spaces and converted the traditional library into collaboration areas for classes, small group work, and individual study areas.

119

The traditional library was converted to a Collaboration Space. They included many options for soft seating that can be arranged into many configurations.

Within the Collaboration Space are several breakout rooms for small group meetings.

The Innovation Studios are 3 classrooms that can be opened to create a larger space. The nesting tables make it easy to reconfigure or clear the space quickly.

The intent of this space is for teachers to take a class out of the normal classroom when working on collaborative projects.

More shared spaces outside of the classrooms. This is a large open area furnished with mobile furniture to change the setting and dynamics that come with a traditional classroom.

FINAL THOUGHTS

If you are reading this book, it is most likely because you've already had ideas to change the learning environments in your space. I hope this book has helped give you the overview of what it takes to implement the change with sufficient detail to help with your journey.

Creating Better Learning Environments was written to be an action plan for educators around the world. We need to do a better job preparing our students for the future.

We hear all the buzz words, from 21st Century Learning, Future Ready Schools, Student Centered Learning, the 4 C's (Creativity, Collaboration, Communication, Critical Thinking) plus many more.

When it comes down to it, we are talking about progress. Making things better, and each and everyone one of us can do this. One step at a time, one space at a time. The mere fact that you are reading this book represents your commitment to the process and makes you a Champion.

Share this book, download the free planning guide, send it to others. This book comes from my passion in creating better learning environments.

If you want additional copies of this to share it with others, just send me a message. My hope is to see the days of straight rows in classrooms coming to end in the near future.

Take the first step and you will find there is a network of professionals to support you on this journey. It only takes one person to start the change, why not it be you?

Kevin Stoller

SOURCES

BY CHAPTER

ADDITIONAL RESOURCES
Download the Planning Guide at
www.kay-twelve.com

PART ONE - HOW WE LEARN
PAGES 17-24

Wagner, Tony, *Most Likely to Succeed*

Quizzes on Learning Styles:
  http://www.educationplanner.org/students/
  self-assessments/learning-styles.shtml

  http://www.learning-styles-online.com/overview/

PART TWO - MATCHING LAYOUTS
TO LEARNING STYLES
PAGES 25 - 45

Cain, Susan, *Quiet: The Power of Introverts in a World
that Can't Stop Talking*

More examples available at *Kay-Twelve.com*

*https://www.edutopia.org/blog/flexible-seating-
student-centered-classroom-kayla-
delzer?utm_source=SilverpopMailing&utm_mediu
m=email&utm_campaign=020817%20enews%20f
lexibleseating%20remainder&utm_content=&utm_
term=fea1hed&spMailingID=16517153&spUserID
=MTk5NTg2MjgxNjc1S0&spJobID=960642843&sp
ReportId=OTYwNjQyODQzS0*

PART THREE - BUILDING A TEAM
PAGES 47 - 69

CASE STUDY
The Wellington School
3650 Reed Road, Columbus, OH 43220
Head of School, Robert Brisk

Brisk, Rob, *TedTalk*
https://www.youtube.com/watch?v=7_rGFfZMJ6Q

CASE STUDY
Plainfield High School
1 Red Pride Drive, Plainfield, IN 46168
Principal, Melvin Siefert

CASE STUDY
The Linsly School
60 Knox Lane, Wheeling, WV 26003
Headmaster, Justin Zimmerman

https://dschool- old.stanford.edu/sandbox/groups/k12/wiki/a23bb/attachments/da611/HFLI_teacher_take-aways_3.0.pdf?sessionID=26dcbd4186155bfea2dd26fef789ff1f2ca793f3

PART FOUR - COLLABORATION
PAGES 71 - 83

https://www.sherwin-williams.com/property-facility-managers/education/styles-and-techniques/sw-article-pro-colorclassroom

Part Five - Implementation

Pages 85 - 99

Case Study
The Presentation School
20872 Broadway, Sonoma, CA 95476
Assistant Head of School, Tracy Walthard

Hare, Rebecca Louise and Dillon, Dr. Robert,
The Space: A Guide for Educators

Part Six - Evaluate & Communicate

Pages 101 - 109

Case Study
Adlai E. Stevenson High School
1 Stevenson Drive, Lincolnshire, IL 60069
Assistant Superintendent, Sean Carney

http://blog.edtechteam.com/2015/05/inspiring-learning-spaces-and-welcome.html

Welcome to Hillbrook from Head of School, Mark Silver!
https://www.youtube.com/watch?v=uwDrnszy4lI

Bonus Section
Part Seven - Shared Learning Spaces
Pages 111 - 122

Case Study
Cincinnati Hills Christian Academy
11525 Snider Road, Cincinnati, Ohio 45249
Head of School, Randy Brunk

https://www.malvernprep.org/page/Academics/Our-Malvern-Curriculum/The-Learning-Commons

http://www.supportingeducation.org/2014/08/01/making-space-combining-maker-space-learning/

Author Biography

Kevin Stoller is Co-Founder and President of Kay-Twelve.com, a leading national distributor of educational furniture, that helps schools, colleges, libraries, and corporations create better learning environments.

Working with hundreds of schools, Kevin is passionate about helping educators think outside the box to focus on individual student needs. He is active in the entrepreneurial community, hosts several podcasts, and leads workshops to help educators improve learning environments.

He earned his Bachelor's degree from Miami University, and Masters in Business Administration from The Ohio State University. His early projects include an undergraduate documentary, *The Commercialization of Michael Jordan*, examining the value of athlete endorsers and their success in advertising campaigns.

Along with his family members in the education community, Kevin has sought ways to incorporate the entrepreneurial mindset into the schools. He routinely participates as a mentor or judge in student business competitions, and coordinated a regional student entrepreneur competition for the Global Student Entrepreneur Award (GSEA).

The host of the podcast, *Better Learning*, Kevin connects a variety of change-makers, ranging from K-12 (Public, Charter, Private & Independent) to higher education and corporate learning. Lessons learned from successful – and failing education initiatives – can often be applied to other environments.

Meanwhile, Kay-Twelve.com continues to grow and was recently named to the *Inc 5000* list of the fastest growing companies in America. Kevin and his wife Darci have three children, Grant, Maggie & Tessa.

This book was intended to be a self-implemented guide to create better learning environments for your organization. If you need guidance, our team at Kay-Twelve.com is available to help. We encourage you to join our community of others that are passionate about improving student outcomes.

Creating Better Learning Environments

www.Kay-Twelve.com

888-624-5451

Kay-Twelve Core Values:

We listen, we care, we follow through

We challenge complacency

We do the right thing

We attract others that share the same passion

We are stronger as a team

Made in the USA
Middletown, DE
01 February 2019